NO MORE FLINCHING

5 STEPS TO OVERCOMING ADVERSITY

To: Bonita
I will
I pray this
Book is an inspiring
read. Carlotta
10/11/19
(601) 918-0091

CARLOTTA TAYLOR

Dedication

This book is dedicated to my grandparents, Frederick Vernon Taylor, Annie Lee Taylor; to my children, Ashanti, Ashton and Tyshawn; my great-grandmother, Mary Gray a.k.a. "Big Momma;" my siblings, Karl, Jr., Rosanna and Joshua; to my high school friends, Tomice Lanier and Wykeisha Mason; to my mother, Rosie Payne, Sr. a.k.a. "Pops"; my favorite instructor at Belhaven University, Dr. Angela Gaddis; to Pastor Sandra Adams, Dr. Eldridge Henderson, my dear friend, Attorney LaDonna Spencer, and last but not least, to Paul Wesley Franks, Jr. for the freedom and the push. To all of my supporters, fans and friends: Thank you all for your inspiration, words of encouragement and the roles you played in making this book possible.

In Loving Memory
of Frederick Vernon Taylor

Table of Contents

Preface

As I drove to a known intersection in Jackson, Mississippi, responding to a lady in need of a ride, after four years of experience, I know that I'm supposed to inform her that police officers do not transport because we are not a taxi cab service. In spite of that, I already had a mind to get her to her destination quickly. After all, we are here to help. Therefore, I used my Officer's discretion.

I pulled up to the scene, exited the car looking around for the female who fit the description I was given. So far, no lady wearing gray colors in sight. I walked around to give a final look before clearing the call and returning to my normal day on the job.

Suddenly, I saw an African-American female inexplicably in the same area. It was as if she appeared out of nowhere. I went to her to question whether she had seen a person fitting the description. She immediately told me the lady just caught the Greyhound.

"Are you sure?" I asked.

"Yes," the woman said. "She just caught the bus, and she was wearing a gray shirt with blue jeans."

Although she was adamant about what she had witnessed, I still looked around. She continued on, saying that the lady was a street walker and that she had seen her face a lot. She knew the woman was involved in drugs and other things.

Then she asked me, "Do you know why I know this?"

"No, why?" I replied.

"Because that used to be me. I used to be on the street, smoking crack, and a prostitute. But I went to church, and the church prayed for me. Now, I'm an evangelist. God healed me and I've been drug-free for years." Those were her exact words to the best of my memory.

"I would have never known," I responded in awe.

I was astonished. She looked healthy and vibrant, revealing no evidence that would connect her to her past life. Her spirit was pure and I felt safe conversing with her.

It was a sunny, bright day. The air was perfect; perfect for a perfect moment.

"You know what? I want to share something with you. I was a victim of child abuse. My father used to beat me to a pulp to where I wore black eyes and bruises to school. I grew up mainly in the Department of Human Services' custody, living in shelters, foster care, going from home to home while also returning to my parents' home. I counted 26 different times I moved from place to place. I tried to commit suicide at the age of twelve. During that period, a light appeared to me and God helped me. And, although I am a police officer, I thank God for bringing me through those difficult times. I have been through a lot, but I thank God for protecting me and keeping me from being on drugs, and on the street, and slipping through the cracks, because that could have been me."

In an instant, time stood still. Angelically, she spoke a word to me I will never forget.

"This call was not for that lady. You are a police officer, used to going place to place, answering different calls for other people, but this call was not for her! God wanted to get your attention," the lady said to me. "He knows that lady is going to be all right. This call was for you. God has a plan for your life; He wants to use you to help others. You are blessed and there are three words God wants me to tell you right now."

As I stood there in full uniform, the dispatcher on the radio as quiet as ever, she repeated three words over and over to me until I broke down in tears, gasping for breath. As if the windows of heaven opened up, God spoke directly to me, saying: "Tell your story."

Tell your story. These words have been echoing in my mind since about 2007, so here it goes.

Chapter 1

Life with Grandma & Grandpa

One of the most difficult questions for me to answer is this: "Where are you from?"

I like to give honest answers. When you've moved around all of your life, what do you say? My answer is, "I've lived all over Mississippi, and I've lived in Michigan for a short time during my early youth." Very lengthy answer. I don't intend for it to be a difficult one, but I moved around so much, I feel I can almost say my name was called on the roll of practically every elementary and middle school in Mississippi.

Carlotta Taylor?

Here.

Finding a starting point for this book was disobliging. I decided to begin during a happy time. Therefore, I pose three questions.

What were you doing at the age of nine?

As a child, do you recall how life was?

Did anything stand out in life for you?

For me, at nine years old, life was the grandest it had ever been. Actually, it's the single best year of my childhood. I lived with my wonderful grandparents, Frederick Vernon Taylor and Annie Lee Taylor, in Hattiesburg, Mississippi. My grandfather was, and is my angel. While I was in their care, I lived in fear. I was afraid that if the doorbell would ever ring, or if there would be a phone call, it would be someone coming to pick me and my brother up to take us back to that awful, dreadful place. That place we called, "The House." I will explain later. But for now, let's enjoy Grandma and Grandpa's house.

It was the most heartfelt place ever on earth. That grayish, bricked house with a little front porch was filled with the aroma of food cooking. Like clockwork, we ate three times a day and dessert was served just before bedtime. There was always the feeling of comfort and cozy. Either the Red Sox game or golf always played on the satellite dish T.V. Grandpa was a golf pro; I didn't know what a "golf pro" was at age nine, but I understand now. One wall alone was heavily decorated with Grandpa's golf trophies. He was an awesome man and my hero.

I learned about Motown recording artists Marvin Gaye and Tammi Terrell. Grandma told us about the time when Marvin Gaye kissed her on the cheek at a concert she attended in her younger days. Yes, Grandma was a fly, ambitious fox, a business lady and a member of Zeta Phi Beta Sorority, Inc.

Whenever it was time for the kids to watch T.V., we always watched shows and movies like *Winnie the Pooh, Mary Poppins, Cabin in the Sky,* and *The Wizard of Oz.* Those shows were often reruns, but they're still some of my favorite shows. Consistency and care were a part of our world for a change. Grandma and Grandpa's house was the place where we got to keep our Christmas gifts. They were really ours to have. I was treated like I was loved. It was the first time I was comfortable with the word "home."

My grandparents rescued my brother and me from being adopted by a family, whom I have no recollection of. They actually showed up in court to stop the proceeding. The details were a little fuzzy, but I remembered the court room and the big smile on my face when the judge made his ruling.

I can still vividly picture the backyard of my grandparents' house on Berkshire Drive. Since adulthood, I'd drive down the road and stare in awe at the now - occupied house, wondering if the people living there knew they were living in a blessed home. The earth sloped from low to high the further I walked away. Grandma planted a neat vegetable garden there. She loved cooking with her vegetables; those green onions and tomatoes were always fresh. We had a wooden tree house that my brother Karl, Jr. and I had to climb up to enter. It was our home away from home. You couldn't tell us we weren't living. Who knew life could be this way, where I could actually breathe and not feel like I was kidnapped? I felt like I belonged.

I was the goofiest little nine year-old. I hated to read, which was often my punishment for being a talker in my classroom. Can you believe at nine, I was given the book, "Return of the Jedi," to read from cover to cover? I sat on that brown sofa and looked at that book, wanting to do a magic trick to be anywhere and do anything but read.

Junior and I would play hide and seek. When our grandparents came home, I would leave a handwritten note where I knew they would see it. They would read it aloud: *"Grandma and Grandpa, me*

11

and Junior ran away. We are never coming back."

They put up a real "big fuss" about us not being there, saying, "Oh my, Fred, have you seen Carlotta and Karl Jr.? They are missing! Where could they be?" I'm sure I wasn't wise enough at nine not to have my shoes protruding from the edge of the couch as I hid behind it with my brother. We giggled to ourselves as they went through the house, calling our names.

I would finally get up and run to them and say, "Here we are!" They knew they made my brother and I feel important. I believe that's why we played like we ran away. Funny how bad things didn't happen to us when we were at Grandma and Grandpa's house. We felt protected. It was so different to feel what love felt like.

My brother, who is two years younger than me, was the smart one. I, on the other hand, was the total opposite. Math, English, and Art were my favorites; all other subjects, I could throw in the trash. Finding joy in reading seemed like an impossible mission, and I was horrible at test taking. I hadn't figured out at that time that I had to adopt a skill of studying in a way that was suitable for me. Needless to say, I brought home horrible report cards while my brother brought home straight A's.

Despite my grades, life was still grand. It was the most exciting it had ever been. The way I looked at it, I would figure out how to become smart at some point in life, but I was still getting used to being a child and doing childlike things without being tormented. Eventually, my younger sister Rosanna was added to our household, special delivery from DHS. That was a shift for my brother and me.

We got all of the attention until then. Our baby sister, who loved to cry, demanded to have her way. My grandmother kept her calm by giving Rosanna one of her own baby dolls she nicknamed "Baby Anna." Rosanna would snatch Baby Anna from Grandma's hands and immediately, her tears dried up.

Oh, the joys of Christmas at Grandma and Grandpa's house! We received gifts wrapped with love, and sealed with shiny bows. Lighted yo-yo's, a train track that choo-choo-ed as it circled the kitchen floor. We had books to read, along with other things. It wasn't long before one or two pieces of the tracks from the train set went missing, causing the train to crash. It was symbolic of the way our life transitioned not long after.

While in our grandparents' care, we attended church regularly. I was astonished at how I was a little girl sipping real wine from a metal cup that was wiped with a cloth once and repositioned for the next church member to sip from. We partook in different programs for children. It was the first time I made "paper"; the first time my brother's shadow was cut and pasted onto cardboard for artwork. We sang songs at church and laughed as we read the hymnals. My brother and I never understood one in particular. We asked ourselves how the entire church sang praises to our baby sister, "Rosanna in the Highest." Here we were, ages nine and seven, trying to figure out how to get on a two-year-old's level. It was years later before we discovered the original lyrics to the hymn were "Hosanna in the Highest." We laughed for years about this memory.

One particular day, I wasn't aware of my teacher contacting my grandparents concerning my behavior in school. I was cutting up, talking and laughing, and thinking I was being funny when I turned around and saw my grandfather sitting quietly in the back of the room. I nearly fainted. I didn't get it then, but I realized that was love. My teacher didn't have any more problems out of me from that day forward.

I loved playing a game we called "cowboys" with my brother in the backyard.

"I'm calling you a draw. Meet me at the saloon, high noon."

We'd say those words aloud in unison, while walking our six steps before spinning around to see who drew their gun first. Our guns were sticks from fallen tree branches. We would talk to our friends through the cracks of the fence in our backyard. I was fascinated with tree bark and how smooth the inside was compared to its rugged outside. The swing set was my next favorite, along with the rocking lawn chair.

Our grandparents told us that we would soon attend Piney Woods and after graduation; we were going to college on a scholarship. Life was all planned out from there. I often daydreamed about how that would play out. Would I make it to college and learn how to make good grades? Maybe Piney Woods would teach me how to be smart. I was afraid of the unknown; yet, I'd rather go there, than go back.

Everything was going smoothly and our lives were on the right track. Things were headed in the right direction, but then it happened. The phone rang. It was out of Grandma and Grandpa's control. Judge's orders. My mother had just given birth to our youngest sibling, and our parents wanted us back for a second chance, which was more like a 50th chance.

I fell to the floor, begging, "Please, please. I don't want to go!" My brother's cries were muted to me because I could only hear my own. I knew he didn't want to go back either. I blinked. Clothes were packed. We kissed all that talk about Piney Woods and scholarships goodbye. Life would never be the same again.

Chapter 2

Back to the House

Doom and gloom took over again. As if the keys to the gates of hell had been recovered, we had to return to the owner. How did we get back here? Who was in control of our fate? Why did this have to happen? Why would the judge send us back? Too many unanswered questions. One fact resonated: I should have known that having a normal life was too good to be true. I should have known it wouldn't last. It was just a matter of time before something bad would happen, as it always did. That's what I got for daring to even think positive.

He was light skinned; he stood at least six feet tall with a thick build and fists the size of Popeye's' after eating spinach. His knuckles protruded from his hands, making his blows intolerable. After so many, I looked forward to the punches because I'd rather have those than a whooping. If that's what we wanted to call it. The only feeling I ever felt around him was fear; fear of getting hit or beaten.

My brother and I would get hit for anything. And by hit, I don't mean a pop on the arm, shoulder, back or leg. I mean literally punched in the face or in the head. The words, "Bring your head here" meant run to him—and by run, you better get there fast and put your head in a position where he could punch you. Sometimes, the punches were more than one or two. I got punched in the face for anything; not moving fast enough to bring him a sandwich or taking too long to make a sandwich. Making any simple mistake would cause him to hit me. He never got tired of punching us in the face. Surprisingly, he only did the oldest two children that way.

I was one of the most picked-on kids at school. Since I was forced to comb my own hair, I went to school looking worse than a hot mess. At the top of the school year, I had enough clothes to make it from Monday through Wednesday. By Thursday, I was re-wearing the shirt I wore Monday with the same black pants I wore Tuesday for the rest of the year. I didn't have any deodorant. I would make the whole class unbearable. One classmate even made up a hideous song about me.

"Carlotta's moving in. You better move out. The funk is kicking strong. It's gonna knock you out!" Some things you never forget. School was a place I hated to go to, but was happy to be away from the house. One day, my teacher escorted me to the bathroom, not understanding why initially. She found some bar soap and wet a few of those hard-brown paper towels in the sink. She handed me the wet paper towels to wash under my arms. I still didn't have deodorant, but that wash up cut some of the odor.

I hated school. It was the place I was judged and scorned. It didn't matter to those kids that I was the product of my parents. Kids bullied me as if I made myself that way. I wanted new clothes. I wanted shoes that fit, and more than one pair. I had long hair; I desired to go to school with the best hairstyles of my era, but I had to settle for the two puff pony tails I wore slighted pinned to the back with barrettes. I never got that middle part straight in the back of my head. I had no one to assist me or show they cared for my well-being and appearance.

I had one friend who wore thick glasses. She lived a few blocks away in the Magnolia Apartments. I would visit her often when I could go outside to play and she would visit me. Since adulthood, I'd never been able to locate her.

The most dreadful school day of all was the day report cards went home. It was Junior's favorite day because, of course, he was always on the honor roll. I, on the other hand, not so much; not even close. I knew how Dad felt about grades. He would force me to stay up for hours, even on school nights. I went to bed at one or two in the morning after massaging his neck, foot, back or hands. And if it wasn't done right, or if I didn't put enough pressure and strength into the massage, hitting the points he wanted, he would say those four words: "Bring your head here."

I hated whenever I was relaxing on the sofa and he would wiggle his foot or hand, or point to his neck, which meant get to massaging. Somedays, I would have rather died than take those few steps across that small living room to touch him. It had to be perfect or his fist was going upside my head.

The walks Junior and I had to the bus stop were long. It would take us 15 to 20 minutes to make a two-minute walk down the street to our bus stop. We dragged our feet and kicked rocks, having our best conversations as siblings on those walks. One day, I begged him to slow down. We already made a quick walk slower than a snail's pace, but I needed us to walk even slower, as if that would help anything.

Report card day had arrived, and there was no hiding anything from Dad. On that day, we made a two-minute walk go 45 minutes. My heart raced. The world was over for me, but I had to keep walking towards that house regardless. My brother feared for me, for we both knew what was coming. However, he still wore a hint of a smile because he knew he would get praised.

As soon as we crossed the threshold of the door, it seemed as though my brother flashed the report card to Dad before I could blink. The joys of having a little brother. Dad did exactly what I knew he would. He went on and on about how smart Junior was. Junior was smart effortlessly. Junior didn't have to study. We didn't get much homework back then, but my oldest brother could listen to the teacher explain what would be on a test and pass it with flying colors after hearing it once.

Dad detected something was up because it took me too long to find my report card. I had to reach down in my backpack to find it, unfold it, then pass it to him. As I was going through the motions, scared as ever, he rushed me to hurry up. He had the report card in his hands. Here it comes.

"You have all D's and F's, and one A in art?" he yelled. "You are stupid! Bring your head here!" He continued his shouting over me, telling me how I was dumb, nothing and so on for quite a while. I became accustomed to getting hit in my face. I was used to it. I would flinch right before the punch landed, bracing myself, getting ready for the pain. I wasn't Daddy's little girl; I was Daddy's little punching bag. Daddy's little stupid dumb child who would grow up to be nothing.

Of all the times she could've come to visit, my one friend chose report card day. She knocked. Dad encouraged me to answer the door.

Dad replied angrily, "What does she want?"

"She's asking if I can come outside."

"No, tell her you can't go outside. Tell her why you can't come outside."

In a mumbling, soft spoken voice, I said, "I can't come outside because I have D's and F's on my report card."

Dad then told me to get on my knees. I had no idea what was about to happen or where this was leading. Get on my knees, now I'm confused. What am I doing? Nevertheless, I did exactly what he said. I looked through the gray, dusty screen door. The door was open, with my best friend on the other side, watching and looking at me while Dad sat in his recliner. I was on all fours on the carpeted floor.

"Now look at her and say, 'I'm dumb,'" my Dad instructed.

I looked at her and said, "I'm dumb."

"Now say, "'I'm stupid!'" he shouted,

"I'm stupid."

"Now, bark like a dog."

I looked at him and then at her, and barked like a dog.

Humiliated, I broke out in tears. Not only was I crying, but so was my friend. Dad had me repeat vile, horrible things. I was dumb, stupid, and wouldn't be anything when I grew up. Over the years, it infiltrated my DNA and became what I thought of myself. It set in.

Each morning of my life felt like a repeated loop. No matter how hard I prayed or wished to wake up to a different life, I was stuck in that house. A white duplex house off Armadale Street in Jackson, Mississippi. Years later, that house was torn down. It should have never been built.

Dad was like a genius; he was extremely smart. He spoke different languages. He had major discussions about any topic. He was musically inclined; he played several instruments, whether it be strings, percussions, keyboard, or piano. Not only could he play by ear, he could read sheet music as well. He had his own band and a lot of the local musicians knew him personally. He spent time with Keith Sweat and Ziggy Marley, two of whom I knew.

At some point, that musician lifestyle took its toll on him, and he got involved with drugs. Drugs could have different effects on people. For Dad, whenever he smoked crack cocaine, it made him extremely paranoid. Ironically, whenever he was high, those were days he never said, "Bring your head here." He didn't beat us or do anything except run to the windows to close them, pace the house, or ask us to check the windows and doors to see if the police were outside. Once we realized the cycle, we were happy when he was high. As children, all we knew was Dad being on drugs equaled Dad not beating on us.

Squeezing a soda can, he would puncture holes in the middle with a pin. Then, using a gutted pen, he would place ashes on the top and heat the can with a lighter as he inhaled the smoke while the white rocks slowly disappeared. But other problems arose.

When Christmas came around, Grandma and Grandpa would bring us gifts. Dad would pawn them in exchange for money to buy more drugs. Mom would go grocery shopping and drop the food off at the house as she went to her second job. Looking back, she worked several jobs just to stay away from the house. She was hardly ever there. Dad would search the trash cans for receipts inside the bags my Mom threw away, just to return the food and use the refund to buy more drugs. Numerous days passed where food was scarce. I ate raw macaroni noodles because there was no pot to cook them. I used to be so hungry, I would chew on my thumb with my back teeth until it tasted like potatoes in my mind. I chewed on my thumb not knowing I was interfering with the growth and form of my teeth. That was a habit of mine for quite some time. Because my teeth were crooked, I only smiled with my lips closed. I was shy and withdrawn and very quiet. But thank God for braces.

Between classes, I didn't know what I was thinking, or what came over me. I was around age 11. I believe I daydreamed a little too hard and when I came back to reality, I was passing my home phone number to one of my male classmates named Thaddeus. Thad was light skinned, built like a football player and had a bubbly personality. It was as if he saw me as a person and not someone to pick on. I believe that's why I lost my mind for a split second and gave him our house number. I don't know if I was trying to be cool or what, but I gave it to him without hesitation.

As I walked away, something kept tugging at me to go back and get the number from him, but I didn't. That decision would cost me heavily. My brother and I took our slow walk to the house as usual. When we got inside, we discovered it wouldn't be a happy day because Dad wasn't on what we called "*dope* dope." Whenever he was on "*dope* dope," we were happy.

I sat in Indian style on the floor across from the table, watching television. We didn't have much furniture, but I was comfortable enough. The phone rang. Dad picked up.

"Hello, you want to speak to who? Carlotta? Here she is."

Dad passed the phone to me. I grabbed it out of his hand as I avoided eye contact with him.

"Hello," I managed to speak.

Thad, without a care in the world questioned, "Can you talk?"

"I can't talk right now," I responded gently.

The instant the phone was placed back on the hook, Dad punched me so hard in my face that I flew onto the floor. That blow popped my eardrum. He stood from his seat, hovered over me and punched me with both fists, calling me a whore. He told me I wasn't going to be anything but a dick sucker when I grew up. He kicked me in my stomach, stomping me like it was a street fight. The pain was unbearable. *I'm his little girl yet he's treated me like...* I can't fathom anything that would make a father do that to his 11-year-old daughter.

23

Rosie Mary was her name. She finally got the courage to speak out. "Karl that's enough, Stop, please!" Mom shouted.

But he kept on. He stopped after a few more punches and kicks.

He screamed, "Get out!"

I wasted no time. I was already fully dressed, I dashed out the door ready to face an unknown world. I took a lot of pain from Dad—mentally and physically. Not knowing how to get to my destination, I went to the nearest phone booth to dial one number I knew by heart. Grandpa always said call him if we needed anything. I jumped off the porch, landed into a sprint and ran away from that house like my life depended on it. I ran fast. Everything flashed before my eyes. I grew more and more excited with every stride. I was almost there. A few more steps, and I would be back to the life my grandparents prepared for me.

Undeniably, I heard a voice, someone shouting with all her might. A lady who never yelled, who never spoke up, was speaking now.

"*Carlotta! Come back.*" I was already deep into the curve. Just a little more, I would be on another street. I was almost there, but not out of her eyesight. I looked back, and it was her, standing alone. One thing I couldn't do was leave Mom. I walked back slowly, slower than I did on report card day.

Dad spoke no words as I entered the house. Mom got me to turn around, but that was it for me. That was the lowest of all lows. There was only one thing to do to fix this. Since life wouldn't provide me a way out, it was time for me to take myself out. I went to the cabinet and grabbed the first bottle of pills my eyes came in contact with. I popped the top and dumped a handful in my hand and took them all. I swallowed and waited. During the wait, I cried out to God. The conversation went like this:

God, why? Why is this happening to me? Please take me away from here. I knew God had to hear me because now I would be close to seeing Him.

A bright light appeared to my immediate right. It was the size of a person. I knew it was an angel. I wasn't asleep. The angel spoke to me, saying that everything would be all right. For the first time, I felt a peace come over me I had never felt before. Nothing happened to me from consuming the pills. I don't know how the pills didn't affect me. Maybe they weren't strong enough or God made a point. A voice told me to hold on a little while longer.

Internally, I comprehended "a little while longer" as when I turned 18 years old. That's when I would legally be able to move out without being mandated to stay with my parents. They would have no choice. I wouldn't have to worry about police saying I was a runaway or the consequences to follow. I would be free, finally.

I was my parents' first-born child. Dad wanted a son first and already had me named Karl, until I was born a girl. He would always tell me he wanted me to be tough, so he taught me how to fight. I had to put my set up, get in proper stance and hit him back. I liked the hitting him back part, and he knew it. He taught me how to swing, how to land my punches and how to shift my weight. He went over everything about fighting with me, down to the last detail. His rule was never hit a person first. If they hit you once, turn the other cheek. If they hit you again, light them up. I think he took those Kung Fu movies he always watched seriously. Bruce Lee was his favorite.

He would call upon kids as they passed our house, saying, "I bet you can't beat my daughter fighting." I never understood that. Couldn't they see I just wanted to be left alone? He would set up a fight for me like that's what I wanted. Yet here I was, scrawny and scared. The last thing I wanted to do was fight other people. After getting hit a few times, it wasn't long before kids' punches felt lighter than mosquito bites.

Junior knew I was strong. I watched my brother engage in his first fight, and he got handled all along the fence. I wanted to jump in to help him, but Dad said it was his fight. I had fought several of my own fights. I was confident even though I fought scared.

I witnessed my brother in another confrontation, with a young girl who got off at our bus stop to fight my brother. One day, my brother screeched to me, "Get her, Carlotta!" Not because she was a girl, but he was scared to fight.

While she tried to get to him, I interceded and said, "If you trying to fight my brother, you have to go through me."

Dad walked outside to witness the fight and took a seat in the perfect spot where nothing blocked his view. I think he enjoyed it. She walked into my personal space, all in my grill. She hit me in my face. I looked towards Dad, remembering his rule. The first punch, let it slide. She hit me again on the other side of my face. I looked at Dad, who nodded, affirming me to let it rip. This fight was too easy. I lost it on her head. I blocked all her swings, landing my punches in all the right places. She didn't want to give up, and she didn't want to lose.

I let her walk away, but she returned with a long stick. She tried to hit me with her newly fetched weapon. I managed to get the stick from her within a matter of seconds. My hands swooped in her scalp, grabbing her hair with the tightest grip ever. Time slowed down as I blocked everything out. I slung her head back, still maintaining my good grip, ready to forcefully smash her head into the corner of my neighbor's concrete porch. Dad jumped up from his seat as he saw what was about to happen next. With all his might, he shouted, "NO!"

In that very moment, jail was waiting for me. How would I ever adapt to that lifestyle? Wasn't that where the dummies, whores and stupid people go? God didn't fail me that time either. I listened to my father and I let her go. She never came back for more.

How could a man who had a bright side, turn into a monster from day to day? Dad would get the whole family out of the house to go on runs. He loved going out to eat at fast food restaurants and laughed often. His social skills were intact. Obviously, other adults thought he was a great father. I never felt safe with Dad no matter what mood he was in. I knew the happy mood wouldn't last.

When Dad wanted us to get out the house, he would tell us to go to the YMCA. He never knew this, but I never went inside. I wasn't going inside to get talked about or laughed at. I had enough of that in school. My brother would go in and I would wait outside.

27

Some days, Dad would tell my brother and me not to come back until we had $20. Since I was the oldest, I had to come up with a way to get $20. I started a raking business, but all the benefits went to Dad. My brother and I would rake yards and make well over $20 and bring my father back every dollar. We didn't mind because when he took the money, he bought drugs.

One afternoon, I walked to the neighborhood store. This older man had been watching me. He touched me in an awkward way, rubbing me on my shoulder, and tried to get me to follow him and leave the store. My brother made it home to tell Dad. Before I knew it, Dad found the guy and beat him so bad, he walked with a limp for years. Dad came to my rescue like my hero. It baffled me how he could be this way when it was someone else treating me badly, and yet, he treated me horrendously. How could the same man who protected me, hurt me?

One night, Dad was out playing with his band. He had a gig and that meant he would be out late. Mom was working her second job as usual. My brother, young and full of adventure, decided he would fire up a cigarette inside the house. After he lit the cigarette, he dropped it on the carpet and a fire started. Within seconds, the house was consumed with heavy smoke. We fought really hard to put the fire out, franticly stomping and fanning the smoke. The fire vanished but the smoke thickened into a dark gray fog.

The smoke wasn't going anywhere. Dad pulled up and it was the calm before the storm. He asked us over and over who did it, and neither of us said a word. Since Dad couldn't get an answer out of us, he decided to beat it out of us. Before he got started, he stuffed the bottom of the doors and windows with bath towels. I knew this would be gruesome. He was making the house sound-proof. He took a 2x4 piece of wood from one of our twin bunk bed frames and hit us hard. He punched us, grabbed a broom stick, and popped us on the top of our head with it. It felt like he broke my scull.

My brother blurted out, "Carlotta did it."

Lord, why?! Dad then turned toward me and went ballistic. I had to think fast. How could I prove it? I remembered our neighbor, who we called Honey-Honey, saw Junior playing with the cigarette. Honey-Honey gave my brother the lighter to light the cigarette. Dad managed to take a break from beating us and went across the street to ask Honey-Honey if what I said was the truth. Honey-Honey confirmed, and Dad went to another level of rage. He was so upset that my brother allowed me to get beaten for him, he tried to make me take my anger out on my brother. He put my brother in a corner and he told me to hit him. I hit him lightly, not wanting to hurt him but wanting to look as if I were being obedient. Even though my brother lied on me, I couldn't do him like that.

Dad screamed in my ear, "If you don't hit him harder, I'm going to get you! I know you can hit harder than that!" I started hitting my beloved brother harder and harder as Dad instructed me to do. My brother cried and screamed for me to stop. How was this the life I was supposed to live? Dad got the iron and pressed it into my brother's head. He threw his head into the kitchen counter. When my brother hurt, I hurt. I felt like I knew what the problem was.

We must have been kidnapped. No dad would treat his real kids like that, and no mother would allow her kids to get beaten to this extent. If I could just escape. Escaping was my dream, but it was just what my brother did. As he climbed out the window the next night, he asked me to come with him. I couldn't. I knew the system wouldn't do anything for us. They always took us out, but they also brought us right back. Ironically, a police officer lived right next door to us on Bow Street. Dad got in the habit of sound proofing the house to muffle the screams. What a life.

When Dad figured out my brother ran away, he flipped out harder than I'd imagine. He even yelled at Mom. It wasn't long before the police brought my brother back to the house. Dad showed no mercy. The police wouldn't help, and DHS didn't either. No matter how upset Dad would get, he never hit Mom with the exception of him slapping her when I was five years old. I'd never forget how the black-eyed peas she was prepping flew all over the floor. Dad shoved my mom into the wall when she tried to speak up again about my brother running away. No one had a voice living in that house except Dad.

When beatings like this occurred, it meant weeks of missing school for both of us. We didn't look suitable for class. We were already accustomed to applying the raw steak and raw sliced potatoes over our eyes or bruised body parts to heal us quicker.

But thankfully, DHS had their own special way of finding out what was going on with us in our parents' care. During our next visit, we were given dolls.

"This one doll is your dad. These dolls are you two," Junior and I were told. "Can you show us how your daddy acts with these dolls?"

We took the dolls and used the main doll that represented Dad to beat the other dolls. We slapped, punched and yanked the dolls around, showing no care, love or concern. It wasn't long before we were back into another foster care home.

Chapter 3

Ms. Hattie Hawk's Farm

From day one, I knew something wasn't right the moment I laid eyes on Ms. Hattie Hawk. She maintained a forced smile when our social worker introduced us to her as our new temporary foster mom. We stood there like little wooden puppets in the dim living room, perfectly foreshadowing our next few months in her care. The only thing I was content with was that DHS managed to keep Junior and me together since there had been talk about us having to be separated. It was hard keeping siblings together. Looking back, I realize DHS won strong arguments to keep us in the same household since we were brother and sister.

Ms. Hattie Hawk deserved an Oscar for how happy she looked to see us. It didn't take long for her to show her true colors. After our social worker left, as quick as one could snap their fingers, the real Ms. Hattie Hawk revealed herself. She was a medium build, dark-skinned elderly woman of few words. She spoke with authority and she was someone you didn't want to try.

She didn't like kids at all. Matter of fact, she hated for us to be in her house. She would tell us to go outside and not to come back in until it was time for bed. I did enjoy the freedom of being outside on the farm all day, but it was very strange not being able to go inside, even when I needed to use the bathroom. She had a family member who lived with her named Chris. Chris had a medium complexion and thin build. His clothing looked like scraps. Chris was younger than us and he was wild. Chris called himself showing my brother and me the ropes. He would go to the side of the house and squat. He would do his business and clean himself with leaves. Junior and I looked at each other in amazement. I knew my brother, we had a telepathic moment. We were both thinking one word: Disgusting.

Chris was very creative in the different ways he used the bathroom outside. He would sometimes climb on top of the roof and let it fall from the sky. We were speechless. I felt very uncomfortable being a young girl doing things outside that I should be able to do inside in private. Even though she ordered us to not come inside, one day, I had a streak of boldness. I walked to the door and asked her to use the bathroom inside one day.

"Go on and use the bathroom, ole long-faced yella gal," she responded in a disgruntled manner. I never knew what to think about her calling me that. It hurt me, but once again, there was nothing I could do about it. Anytime she needed me, that's what she would call me. Those words hurt just as bad as being called dumb and stupid. Ms. Hattie Hawk's house was on a farm packed with pigs, chickens, horses and cows. Junior, Chris and I were very familiar with the pigs. When it came time for her to get her food, she would load us up in the truck. Back then, we rode in the back with no seatbelt. To describe the first run, she would drive up to the back of grocery stores and pull up to a small window. The person at the window would ask her what she needed the food for, and Ms. Hattie responded, saying that she needed it for her hogs. They would give her tons of food, all mushed and mixed together, and she would dump it in a barrel.

When we got back to the farm, we would hop off the truck, and she would tell us to get our share of food first. My brother and I were in complete disarray. What did she mean, "get our share?" Without hesitation, Chris dug in, picking out cinnamon rolls, Little Debbie snacks, and food that didn't look as molded. My stomach was weak. Most of the food was mixed together, outdated and molded in most places. We were forced to choose what we would eat out of the slop she fed her hogs. We went on several runs afterwards. Each time was equally disgusting.

We couldn't wait until our social worker came to visit us again to ask us how we were doing. God intervened before that was possible. One day, Ms. Hattie walked into a store and left Junior and me inside the car for too long. We almost died of heat exhaustion. We made the news and once again, we were on our way back through another endless cycle of going to the shelter, foster home and back to the house.

Often times, we lived in the shelter between transitions. It was the best option outside of living with our grandparents. However, eventually, the shelter life became a revolving door. They treated us in such a manner where it appeared we had exceeded our stay. I loved the fact I had my own toothbrush, toothpaste and mouthwash. Even today, opening brand-new mouthwash often takes me back to the first time I had my first bottle in a shelter. I had toiletries, clothes and even pajamas. I first learned how to play video games there as well. My favorite game was *Mario Brothers*. I loved watching the cartoons in the morning time, *Smurfs* and *Jem*. Everything was on a strict schedule, and we went to bed super early.

For the umpteenth time, our social worker transported us to yet another foster home. Ms. Owens' house was a little different. It was our absolute favorite foster home of them all. Ms. Owens was a nice woman with a medium-complexion. She made sure me and Junior were treated nicely. Her daughter's name was Tonya, who was also really nice to us. They made sure we were fed, bathed and clothed properly. There was a nice homey feel at Ms. Owens' house. There was almost nothing bad to say of our stay there except this one day; it was someone's birthday. Everyone was excited and getting dressed to attend. Junior and I knew we weren't going because we weren't getting dressed. We were left sitting in the living room to watch T.V. Before long, everyone was heading out the door with their big smiles, in anticipation of having a good time. All of them belonged to a family, their presence mattered; Junior and I sat staring at a television screen, feeling abandoned. At that moment, I realized that no place was truly safe.

The cycle continued. Junior and I traveled from home to home. As we went door to door, the rap sheet of who we were, where we came from and our experiences were discussed before the initial greeting. One lady in particular, whose name I don't recall, made me feel eerie and weird. She touched me in the wrong place, positioned me on top of her and did things I knew she shouldn't have done. I was glad when she stopped.

A lot of my memory was suppressed and resurfaced like flashes sometimes. I'd tried to make myself forget most tragedies. I tried to force my memories away because some of them are too horrible to think of, but some were too gruesome to forget.

Chapter 4

Back Again

Sitting on pins and needles, holding my breath, feeling stressed, anxious and frightened perfectly described my feelings anytime I was around my Dad. Nothing was new with report cards. Junior had straight A's. I had C's, D's, F's and an A in art. My teachers felt sorry for me coming to school with broken arms, black eyes and bruises. They just passed me along from grade to grade. There was no way I could have passed every grade with the F's I earned. Dad was heavy on the drugs those days and much lighter on the beatings. We had already experienced Mom having a nervous breakdown throughout the years, and Dad got shot in the leg six times from an encounter with a crazy man. I remember the hospital staff rolling him in on a stretcher, his leg wrapped in black-trash-bags, as they rushed him into surgery. I had hoped he didn't make it through. I knew I was in a horrible place to wish those kinds of things about my own father.

One day, he sat in his favorite recliner after eating some chili. Moments later, he started coughing uncontrollably.

"Carlotta!" he yelled. "Did you poison me?"

I looked at him and said, "No."

Immediately after I answered him, I wondered why I didn't ever think of that. I remember thinking at the age of twelve, I wish I had.

Turned out, he just had food poisoning. It must have been a bad can of chili.

Dad didn't care about DHS. He'd cuss them out and tell them he would still discipline us. They were afraid of him. We had no hope even with the police living right next door to us. The officer never said anything about a disturbance. He never came to our rescue.

Mom had been spending a lot of time away from the house. She would walk out the house dressed like a model off to hit the runway. She had an athletic build with long, natural, flowing hair down to her hips. Her skin was beautiful, and she had nothing on her face but a hint of lipstick. She always smelled fresh. One day, she went to the mall and purchased over $200 in makeup from Fashion Fair cosmetics. I figured she wanted to be even fancier.

The next day, she got up early to make up her face. She cried her eyes out because she couldn't apply the makeup. I knocked on the door and I told her I could do it. I had never applied makeup before. I figured since I could draw, and was good in art, of course I could make up Mom's face. I was right. I painted her face to perfection—from the foundation, to the eye shadow, liner, mascara, blush and lipstick. I did it all, and it looked magnificent. The following months ahead, making up my Mom's face was my job before school, which was something I loved doing.

Mom would hardly ever be home during the rough times. As I got older, I became more aware. Mom was the only person, besides Junior, who I was comfortable talking to. I felt so much relief going to work with her. I learned Mom was doing personal home assistance work after her full-time job with a man named Mr. Lablonc.

Mr. Lablonc lived in a nice, huge house, made of a dark wood. I had never been inside a nice house like that, other than my grandparents' home. Mr. Lablonc's arm had been amputated from the elbow down. That was the first time I had ever laid eyes on an amputee. He used these mechanical artificial arms that pinched at the end like a clamp. He appeared to be really nice, and I ate well at his house. On a random day, Mom left to go to the store. Mr. Lablonc asked me to put baby oil on his legs. As I was rubbed the baby oil in, he asked me to place it on his genital area and do other inappropriate things. I knew what he asked me to do was wrong, so I walked out his room and left him lying there. He followed me to the bathroom and knocked on the door, asking me to lift my shirt and show him my breasts. He said if I did, he would give me some money.

As soon as Mom returned, I told her what happened. She told me that she would take care of it, and I didn't have to come back anymore. My other siblings took turns going to Mr. Lablonc's house. Although I didn't want to return to Mr. Lablonc's house, I didn't want to stay at home either.

Dad and his lady friends were friendly with each other. He would flirt with one of his singers in his band in front of us. The house would be packed with different people and it reeked of incense and marijuana. Junior and I would hit the door to walk around the neighborhood. A few times, Junior and I went with Mom after she worked her primary job. I believe she kept us away from the house to prevent us from getting beaten. I'll never forget the day Dad accused us of eating too much food from a dish he made. He ate half and wanted the four of us to split one plate and leave a large amount for Mom who hadn't made it home. Of course, we were hungry and ate a little more, but it wasn't that much of a difference. When she arrived home, there was little to no food left for her. He started to whip us for eating her share, but Mom spoke up and said she got it and called us back in the room. She took out her belt and told us to cry loud like she was hitting us. She was actually hitting laundry clothes that were in garbage bags. Mom wasn't perfect, but we knew she didn't stand for the abuse. We truly appreciated our Mom for helping us out that day.

Although I didn't want to accompany her when she went to Mr. Lablonc's house, she had an associate named Mr. Robert. Mr. Robert drove an old model tan Grand Marquis that smelled like old, stale peanuts. Mr. Robert established himself as being a friend of Mom's and that she was someone who helped him because he was old. After he saw me a time or two, he felt like he knew me. Around 1992, Mom told him I would try to make the honor roll. He told me and my mom at the same time that I would never make the honor roll. When he said that, I felt like a failure before even trying. He made it hard for me to ever forget he said that to me. Mr. Robert was cool and creepy at the same time. The more we frequented his home, the more he got comfortable with me. He once asked me to allow him to do something to me for two dollars, and again, I told my mother. That was the last time I went with her to her other jobs.

It seemed like it was taking forever for my 18th birthday. I had six whole, long years to go before stepping out into the world. Thank God, a change in the weather came early. Mom came to me for everything. She shared with me that we were leaving Dad. I was so happy. However, a part of me thought she was playing, just to get a reaction. The look in her eyes proved to me she was serious. Over the next couple of days, we packed our clothes in black plastic bags as if we were going to do laundry. We had several packed bags in every room all around the house. Luckily, he never noticed the bags.

The day came when it was time to make a run for it. We spent about a week preparing for this day. The plan was well thought out and very strategic. Dad happened to be sleeping in his favorite recliner that morning, fully reclined and snoring. We carried the bags out one by one, and he never opened his eyes. We moved in silence, holding our breath as we tiptoed through the house. This was a life or death case in my eyes. If he woke up and realized what was happening, we would see the worst of Karl Taylor, Sr. He didn't wake at all the entire time. We successfully moved everyone and all the bags of clothes out the house.

I gasped for air as I rode in the car. We were headed to my mother's home town, Brookhaven, Mississippi. I stared at the house ensuring that there was no sign of him running out the house to chase after us. We got as far as one block. Mom parked the car, and I look at her with the words, "What's wrong?" written all over my face.

"I left my purse," she whispered. "My driver's license and all my money is in my purse."

She had to go back. Disappointed, I dropped my head. No way

could she drive back, get her purse without him waking up, and him beating us all to death. However, Mom had a better plan. Instead of driving back, she got out the car and walked back to that house. We waited right there timorously, just as still as those plastic bags full of clothes. We didn't move a muscle; we just waited.

That was the longest walk in history to me. I watched her walk down the street. As she made a right, we could still see her through the wire fence across the lawn. It felt like forever waiting to learn whether she was okay or not.

Time stood still until she finally walked out the house. I made sure I watched her back to make sure he wouldn't sneak up on her. Mom walked away and never looked back. She made it with her purse in hand and off we drove to Big Momma's house.

I had no idea we were getting dropped off. Mom gave us a big hug, and we didn't see her until next year. At least she didn't leave us in his care—that was better than abandoning us altogether. I figured she needed some time to get herself situated. Living with Big Momma was great. We got one dollar in food stamps every single day to go to the store. Back then, we could buy a lot with one dollar. Big Momma was the best cook ever. She would save up her money throughout the year to buy everyone really nice gifts for Christmas and birthdays.

That year, I was in the seventh grade and I made friends. Making friends was easier when I was actually in one place for the entire year. Even though I was the oldest, I could be a regular 13-year-old. Big Momma didn't make me solely responsible for my siblings like I was their babysitter. That's what I had been taught. I was the oldest and had to teach my siblings what to do. Often times, when I lived with Dad, I would get whippings if my siblings did anything crazy. Dad would tell me if they did something wrong, they got it from me. So, when they got a whooping, I got it, too just because. Thank God those days were over.

Big Momma would have cookouts at her house every holiday and the food was superb. The house was packed, and there was nothing but compliments of how great grandmother should open her own restaurant. It didn't matter what time it was, if Big Momma was hungry, she would get up and cook a full-course meal. Chicken and dumplings from scratch, collard greens, cornbread, roast, pecan pies and more, if her heart desired. She taught me the importance of enjoying what you work for, and if you want something in this lifetime, get what you want and don't settle.

Big Momma bought me my first black, snake-skinned purse and my first white Coach purse. I wore name-brand clothing and purses before I knew what name brand meant. Big Momma bought most of my clothes as Walmart special.

Aunt Helen wasn't too fond of me. She told me I would be pregnant by the time I turned 15. Although I had a few close calls, I was never intimate with anyone that young. I was too afraid to do anything. Mom told me if I kissed someone, I would get pregnant. I wasn't taking any chances.

My brother and I had fun. We met a few friends, and I had already mapped my life out now that I was living in Brookhaven. I decided I would go to the same high school Mom did, Brookhaven High. Just when I was adapting to my surroundings, my mom picked us up soon as school was out.

Chapter 5

Life After Dad

Even though we moved into a nice apartment in Madison, Mississippi, there was nothing more I wanted than to return to Brookhaven, finish middle school, and attend Brookhaven High with my new-found friends. But Mom wasn't having it. When I lived in Brookhaven during my seventh grade year, it was the first time I had groups of friends who all seemed genuine and my first boyfriend. I received a letter from someone I liked immensely, but my mother strongly discouraged me in writing back. Distraught, I wept every night for a whole year.

That decision placed a little strain on our relationship for me. However, essentially, we were the best of friends. Mom would confide in me for many things, as if I were a counselor who gave excellent advice. I later learned it was by the grace of God I spoke with clarity and substance. If I didn't learn anything from all I went through, I learned some common sense. With Dad not being in the house, I was always paranoid about break-ins. I felt the world wasn't safe. While everyone else slept soundly in their beds, I prepared my bed with a blanket and a pillow on the living room floor, just in front of the door. In case anyone ever attempted to break in, I would be right there with my knife under my pillow, ready to attack the burglar and send him running.

Everything progressed along just fine until, we moved into a new house in south Jackson. On the way in, my siblings and I noticed some extra furniture inside and, a light-skinned, tall, slender man. His occupation was a truck driver. I guess he was the reason Mom ultimately got the courage to leave Dad, but it was never said aloud. They must've been dating and just took a while before involving the kids into the picture.

I never got close to Fred. He carried himself in such a manner where it seemed he was always up to something. He had this sneaky, lingering eye. It took me a while to figure him out. He never talked much. He would get his food and go in the room with Mom. He kept Mom in the room like he was blocking her from us. Mom and I went from being super close, to me having to repugnantly knock on the door and ask permission from Fred to talk to her or ask her in front of him whatever I wanted. Going from an abused little girl to Dad being replaced with a snake was disheartening.

I prayed for Mom to see his true colors. Anytime I looked in Fred's direction, he was already staring at me. One time when Mom wasn't home, I walked by their room, and door was cracked open. I saw him stretched out on the bed, bare-chested with a brown towel wrapped around his lower body, but his private part was in plain view. I told Mom. I was getting of age, and Mom's friend Claudette was in her ear. She had already received bad advice, insinuating that I liked Fred in the wrong kind of way. But I never lied to Mom nor did I know why she would ever think that of me. That was a very vulnerable and hurtful place to be when my own mother didn't believe in me.

Several other displeasing things happened in that house concerning Fred. He whipped my little sister, and I knew that was a big problem. He had his own five-year-old daughter at the time. Whenever he whipped his daughter, he simply popped her on the hand. However, when he whipped my eight-year-old sister, he took her panties off. Dad got wind of this information and found where we were staying. Within days, he was at our front door, with a gun ready to blow Fred's head off, but it served him right. He got the picture and never laid hands on my little sister again. It felt good having Dad come to our rescue.

Junior realized Fred was a huge problem to our family without Dad. Junior found a crack-pipe in the bathroom and said it was Fred's. Fred had Mom to send Junior away to a house for alternative children. That was the worst thing to do to my brother, who had already been through so much. My heart ached for my brother. I made sure I stayed in my lane so I wouldn't be sent away next. I missed my brother deeply, but grew to live life without him in the picture.

During these years, we still moved around a lot. From Rosa Scott Middle School/Madison Central, to Wingfield and lastly, Forest Hill. Attending Rosa Scott was eye opening. It was a different brand of ball. I'm not sure how I ended up in a speech class, but it was greatly needed because I was no speaker. I was full of stage fright; I would shake and stutter, attempting to utter anything in front of a crowd. I hated my own voice, especially since I never had a voice. Being a part of a new atmosphere allowed me to experience new things.

In the ninth grade, I learned and recited my first poem by Henry Wadsworth Longfellow, *A Psalm of Life*. I know the first four lines from memory:

"Tell me not in mournful numbers, Life is but an empty dream! For the soul is dead that slumbers, and things are not what they seem."

Learning that one poem taught me a lot about pronunciation. I learned so much due to having an immaculate teacher. My high school years seemed to fly by. At age 15, I needed money for clothes. I knew the legal age to work at McDonalds was 16, but I lied and got hired. I was making about $180 every two weeks but had to give Mom $160 to pay the light bill after bragging on what I was making. Needless to say, I never bragged on how much I made again.

I kept to myself mostly. Quiet and shy, I didn't make friends too easily. I wasn't popular. I worked a job, but didn't know what to do with my money. I used to dress like a tomboy. I wore jeans, button-down shirts and Timberland boots. The last thing you would catch me wearing was a dress or a skirt. I enjoyed keeping my hair done. Mom assisted with the upkeep. Every two weeks, I was in Ms. Geraldine's chair. At age 16, I got my first perm, haircut and color. Shaved in the back, long in the front, and blonde was the new me. I looked like I could have been a fourth member of TLC.

I focused on my grades more and figured out how to make good grades. My method for studying was to write and verbally repeat the information over and over until it stuck. Learning and making good grades didn't come easy for me, I had to work for it. But at least I figured it out.

We left Dad back in Jackson, Mississippi, but the flinching never stopped. I didn't only flinch when Dad would swing his fist toward my face or hit me my body. I would flinch merely at someone standing beside me, raising their hand in school. If I was sitting down in the cafeteria at lunch, and a student sitting next to me reached for an item across the table, I would flinch unconsciously. It was something I couldn't control, but wished it would stop.

I had very few friends in high school. I was fascinated with the Army uniform and loved the structure JROTC offered. I hurriedly signed up for that class. I was a member of the Beta Club and National Honor's Society. I danced on the drill team and played tennis during those four years. I recall telling myself I would never join the Army in real life. I was working on myself, yet I was housing all the trauma from my childhood.

I'll never forget the day I confided in my friends, Tomice Thomas and Wykeisha Mason. There were vibrant young ladies. I shared with them some of the things I had experienced. That was the first time I revealed any of it, and it brought me to tears. Surprisingly, they told me they would have never known had I not said anything. They cried just learning about what I had been through. Releasing those tears after all those years was therapeutic for me. I'm thankful to have friends who sympathized with me. Those two really cared, because when I needed them, they were there.

One night, I came in the house about 45 minutes late from work after getting off around 10:00PM. Mom was waiting for me, and although I hadn't had a whooping from her in years, initially she told me Fred was going to whip me. Already knowing Dad wouldn't allow that, he still stood there as if that's what he was about to do. I made it clear he couldn't touch me. Mom then compromised with me and stated she was going to whip me instead, but if I was going to be in her house, then I had to go by her extremely strict rules. I couldn't talk on the phone to boys or girls, even as a senior in high school. The only place I could go was work or practice after school. I never understood that, seeing as how Mom would tell me stories of how she talked to her friends all night long growing up in school. I stood there firmly and told her I wasn't getting whooped by either one of them. Mom looked at me and said if I couldn't abide by her rules I should pack my stuff and hit the door. At age 17, I packed my bags and never looked back.

Chapter 6

Life on My Own

I hadn't graduated from Forest Hill just yet. I was still in twelfth grade and needed to live in the same area to get to school. My high school best friend, Wykeisha, nicknamed "CoCo," asked her mom and dad to allow me to stay with them for a while and they agreed. So there I was, with my bags of clothes, moving in. I ate well and had lots of fun in that little white house on that hilly corner of Raymond Road. I even went to prom there. Although I was out of Mom's house, and was no longer in shelters or foster care, I still lived in the shadows of someone else's family.

After a few months, it became awkward for me to be there. I had to pack up and make a move. I had already talked to my other friend Tomice, and she and her mom welcomed me into their home while I finished my senior year. After graduation, there was no place for me to go but college. I had a really good stay with Tomice, and they treated me like family as well. My next stop was Tougaloo College.

I attended Tougaloo with dreams of going to Spellman. But, I wasn't used to living out my dreams. I never identified what my dreams would be, so settling was easy. But even settling for attending Tougaloo was a miracle. When I filled out the application, I didn't believe I would get accepted. Just getting the acceptance letter startled me.

I had no knowledge of what direction to take in life. I was just going through the motions of what I thought I should do. I didn't know much about college. I was never asked what I wanted to be growing up. Questions like that never crossed my mind. I was focused on other things like praying not to get a black eye and that God would rescue me from that house.

When Mom had us attending Pilgrim Rest Missionary Church in Madison, Mississippi a few years ago, I came to know a wonderful lady and mentor named Rosie Thompson. She took me under her wing and conspired with Mom to make me a Zeta Phi Beta debutante. That's where the first thoughts of Tougaloo College were imprinted in my mind. I still remember Ms. Thompson spending $100 on an ad to sponsor me as a debutante. I admired her for thinking and considering me. I wasn't familiar with Greek life. I was just moving forward.

My first semester at Tougaloo College was very telling. I never knew how to balance freedom and work, because I never had freedom. Deep inside, I didn't feel I had what it took to graduate. I couldn't see myself crossing the finish line. The four years of consistency it would take seemed impossible to me, especially when I didn't know how to be consistent. I had no track record of consistency. I hung out with my roommates and neighbors. One was a cheerleader whose name I can't recall. She was athletic, but she smoked. She made smoking look cool. Another one was a young lady named Ava, who appeared to come from a rich family from Troy, Michigan. Her family sent her plenty of money per month for shopping, but Ava mainly shopped, got weed and stayed high. My roommate appeared cool, but she was sneaky and enjoyed pranking people. She played one prank too many, acting as if she was with the FBI. She tried to inform us our neighbor across the hall was a spy. We fell for the prank and I couldn't take her serious after that. During that semester, I attended one party with that crew around Halloween. We ended up stranded, walking in the middle of the night. Some suspicious looking people followed us. I'm not sure how we got there, but I vowed to God that if He got me out of that situation, I would stop making silly mistakes.

I completed one semester with good grades. I didn't have any support like my roommates did with their parents bringing them food and money. I had to find a place to stay between the breaks because I had no place to go. I brainstormed for a while but couldn't come up with a better option for shelter and pay than joining the military. Scared out of my wits' end, more than I'd ever been, I rode a bus to St. Louis to begin basic training. When I left the military station in Mississippi, my bus ticket was given to a guy named Patrick who was heading to Missouri with me. I was puzzled as to why my recruiter gave him my ticket as well, but I went with it. We wound up sitting in the same seat and became good friends. He ended up being my best friend within that next year of training.

Basic training was very strict. If I could sum up my experience, it was "Dad on steroids, minus the physical beatings." The exercise wore me down just as bad. I got in trouble a few times for passing notes. A few people got kicked out for inappropriate relationships and another for getting pregnant.

Technical Engineering Specialist was my job description. To have that job, I had to be good in math and couldn't fail a test twice, or I would get shuffled back through under another job description. Everything was stressful, and the stress was at a high level. The most agonizing thing for me was the gas chamber. I hated going through the chamber, taking off my gas mask and breathing in those chemicals. But enduring basic training was my only way to survive.

I was a free spirit; I was trying to find my way and had no clue where to start. After graduating from the military, I returned to Tougaloo College, the only place I had waiting for me. As a gift for graduating from the military, my grandfather purchased my first car. It was paid for, and it was in my name. But, it came with no instructions. All I knew how to do was put gas in it. At that point in my life, I was reaching, for anything, trying to find a grip.

The only person in my corner during this time of my life was Pat. He attended USM. We saw each other every single day, even though we commuted an hour and a half each day one way. We got an apartment together and within the first two weeks, Pat asked me to marry him. Because my mother was heavy in the church, she wasn't with shacking. It was either get married or be homeless. I knew he cared for me more than anyone I had ever known, so I figured I was safer going that route. I was scared, but I did it.

In a ceremony held after Bible school one Wednesday, I wore a khaki skirt, a black shirt with sheer sleeves, and micro braids. As the pastor spoke, I heard a calm voice say, "Turn around and walk away." But, I didn't obey it.

Paralyzed and unable to escape, my mind held me hostage. I reminded myself, either marriage to my best friend or become homeless. Pat previously told me he wanted to marry me and that he didn't want to wait. He gave me an ultimatum: If I didn't marry him then, we couldn't be together. Later that evening, I was on my knees on the kitchen floor, crying uncontrollably, saying that I regretted doing it. Pat listened and told me to give him two years, and he would help me change my mind. I had learned he was trustworthy over the years, so I calmed myself and decided to do just that.

I had to go away for annual training in the military to Fort Polk. While I was there, I learned that my beloved grandfather had passed. I saw him before he got too sick; I just hoped he wouldn't die. I didn't want to believe it, but I couldn't stop it from happening. The last thing my grandfather said to me as I rubbed his head was that he didn't want to die, and he broke out crying. That saddened me deeply. While visiting him, I asked him for advice.

"Grandpa, what would you tell me about this life?"

"Live your life with no regrets and get all the education you can." I kissed his forehead as he cried tears of regrets. I wasn't there for the funeral services where he was honored as a WWII Veteran.

The next six years were spider-webbed crazy. Full of great times, horrible times, growing, learning, backward steps, leaps, more backward steps, more mistakes over and over again. Had I known who I was, I could have made the relationship much better. I threw away my marriage, not knowing what I had and what a marriage truly was or its value.

During this period of my life. I floated through the years and let life happen to me. I lived moment by moment, being tossed here to there. I worked several jobs and would quit them all. From working at Kroger, attending cosmetology school, truck driving school, working at Walmart, Xerox, Roses, Bumpers, just to name a few. I quit them all within three weeks, some within three days.

Three months after being married, I was pregnant with my daughter. That was a happy moment. After she was born, I decided to get more serious about sticking with a job longer than a few weeks for self-development, even though I was told I didn't have to work. I got hired at a golf shop called Dancing Rabbit as a clerk. I worked there for longer than 12 months, the longest job I ever had. I was excited about that. However, one thing that bothered me was that I was ready for a career. I had tried so many things and none of them stuck. But I knew I wanted to do something important in life. And I wanted to do something that paid more than $8.10 per hour.

It appeared to me trying to find my career field was more difficult than I could imagine. I wanted to be successful. I thought about going to nursing school, but I was too afraid of needles. I tried college a few more times since Tougaloo, but would stop after the first class because I couldn't see myself completing. I didn't think great things could happen for me. But I still pressed my way and kept moving. Sometimes it felt like any direction would do long as I kept moving.

I couldn't count how many job applications I filled out. I was looking for anything that paid good money. I applied for two positions around the same time and finally got hired for both of them during the same week. I got hired with the Nissan plant in Canton, MS, and I got hired with a Police Department. I had a decision to make. Which one would it be?

Chapter 7

My Career Field

It didn't take long to think this through; work like a robot on a line or become a police officer. Having military experience was an asset to my decision-making process. If I could go through basic training, I could go through anything. Police officer it was. One thing I was shocked to learn after becoming a police officer was I didn't have Pat's support, but of course, I did it anyway. I went in head first with my expectations set way too high.

Initially, I presumed being a police officer was similar to being in the military. Soldiers got your back, like family. I thought police officers were like a band of brothers and sisters. I later found out that wouldn't be the case for me. In the police academy, I went there to do what I set out to do—graduate, preferably at the top of my class, and do well. I wanted to show that I would make an excellent officer. I was already used to being an overseer, especially since I practically raised my siblings. I felt those things would count for something. I was used to being the disciplined and mature one, as well as the mediator. After a few days in the academy, I thought it would be a piece of cake.

I didn't factor in one unforeseen occurrence that would spring up in my training that wasn't on the curriculum. I was sexually harassed by a tact officer who trained me. I did nothing to warrant this behavior, yet with it, rumors spread about me and the academy's administration treated me as if it were all my fault. Even after their investigation clearly shown my innocence, my name was black-balled as if I were a "sexual harassment complainer." However, the truth was that I never filed sexual harassment, although I should have. I didn't because I didn't want anyone to ever say I did it because I couldn't pass the academy. My mindset at 23 was in the wrong place, worried about the wrong thing. I wanted to make a difference and be a good officer, but that was taken away from me. Things always came the hard way for me. I should have just stood up for justice. But with no support system and no one to have my back outside of Pat, I felt isolated. I chose to stand up for a department and chose to be an officer for a department that never showed me they appreciated me in return.

During the academy, we had a break every weekend and could go home to stay. Early on, it was hard to find a baby-sitter for my young daughter. Mom's boyfriend wouldn't allow my toddler to come in the home because she would start crying, as all babies did. She had divorced Fred, but this new boyfriend told me he didn't allow crying babies in his house, and my baby had to leave. I resented Mom during that time. During this phase of life, I was abandoned by family with only one person to depend on. I felt she should have stood up for me. I experienced family issue after issue during my weekend breaks from the academy, and would show up for training like nothing was wrong and fight my way through. There were moments I was unsure if I could complete my training. I gave it all I had because I could not afford not to graduate. I had too much to lose. Thankfully, I was blessed to have a friend of the family named Rose Dorsey who allowed me to live with her temporarily while I was in training.

Once the news was out at the academy about the tact officer's misconduct, my training switched to nothing but a mental game from there. I toughed it through. I didn't have to guess if they were trying to make me quit. They spelled it out for me. I was chosen by a news anchor to share a few words as to why I wanted to be a police officer. My exact words were, "Because I want to make a difference." I ended up turning in a journal to the staff at the academy filled with each occurrence that described how the officer made me uncomfortable.

The next day during the academy, the training officers repeated my words from the journal I turned in. They mimicked, "So, you want to make a difference," as we stood at the position of attention, waiting for their next command. Everyone knew they were talking about me, and so did I. They made us go outside in the heat, and stuffed us with water for over an hour until some trainees threw up. I was smart enough to fake letting the water go down my throat because I later learned people have died from consuming too much water.

Any other female I know would have quit. His buddies did everything they could to intimidate me and to force me to quit, yet they didn't know I had already been through "Karl Taylor Senior's Academy." If I made it through that, trying to make me quit wouldn't work. I knew with God all things were possible. Even with little to no support, being a police officer was what I wanted to do, and I did it.

After graduation, I was assigned to a precinct. During training, one of my field training officers confided in me and told me a female sergeant told them not to trust me. It was rumored that if any male spoke to me, I would file sexual harassment charges on them. This was defamation of character at its finest, from the police department I chose to work for. Moving forward, everything was an uphill battle, just like my life had been previously.

Around 2005, Pat and I divorced. I felt it was something I needed to do. Looking back at how our wedding day was, I honestly believed I was wrong for being with someone I only saw as my best friend. I felt I could never love him the way he loved me. I felt like he deserved more. Relationship wise, I was acting out. I felt like I couldn't breathe unless I got out of that marriage. I felt trapped. Neither of us were on our best behavior during the entire marriage.

Once the divorce was done and the dust settled, I realized he was gone. I grieved for a long period of time, not realizing what I had done. I went through a period of hallucinating, thinking I would see him walking around the corner or talking. After being with someone for eight years, to going to straight stillness and quiet, that was a very difficult time. With no guidance, I didn't know which step to take. Regret set in for some time. The worst thing I could have done was get involved with someone else.

Within a matter of weeks, I went to the mall, walking into my favorite store, The Limited and I heard a voice pay me a compliment.

I looked back and saw this young-looking kid. Initially, I paid him no mind. But he repeated himself again, handed me his number and asked for mine. In a split second, I gave him my number. My first mind told me to throw my number off by one digit, but I didn't. I asked him how old he was for grins. To my surprise, he was my age. I still wasn't interested in him. That day, I left the mall to get ready to work my part-time job at Walgreens. I never would have called him. I decided not to entertain the thought; but that night, I received text messages saying things like, "I'm trying to talk to you, but you won't give me the time of day." Only because I was bored, I texted back and allowed him to come to the Walgreens parking lot to keep me company during my break.

I was gullible. I never received any advice from my father about how to be in relationships or what to look out for in men. And since I had just broken up with someone I had my first long-term relationship with, I figured all men treated their significant others the same way Pat treated me. Boy, was I wrong. It was uncanny how I didn't learn the value of my marriage until after we divorced. If a relationship could ever be karma from treating someone bad, this guy was King Karma to me. This was my first bad relationship and I stayed in it two years too long. One blessing from this destructive situation was my son, Tyshawn, born in 2008. To this day, his father has only seen him once at the age of nine for a publicity stunt on Facebook. He was two years old the time before that. I could literally look back on pictures I took during this relationship and noticed how I looked much older than I do now. That's just how stressful being with someone who doesn't cherish you can affect your looks and well-being.

While I suffered in the relationship arena, I thrived and buried myself in my work. I dug hard to focus and not allow anything to get in my way, even a bad relationship. It was tough, but that's how I held myself together. 2008 was the year I pledged Delta Sigma Theta Sorority, Inc. and completed my associate's degree, even with my youngest sons' father being wayward and doing his own thing. It was stressful, but I refused to allow him or anyone to distract me from my goals.

I spent a few years on patrol. Two times, I went before a panel to interview for detective but wasn't selected, even though I knew with confidence I did excellent. About a year or two later, a new chief was selected. Chief McMillian's administration replaced the entire division. I interviewed for one of the slots that was open. The day after my interview was the day before my due date. Nine months pregnant, I was selected for the position. My title went from being a police officer to child protection detective, also known as sex crimes. After my six weeks were up, I was back at work, in my office.

As a new detective, working on child abuse cases and crimes against children I felt this was my calling. I thoroughly enjoyed solving cases and making sure people who did bad things to children would get the justice they needed. After about six months in this field, a witness to a case I was working asked me if my last name used to be Taylor. I told him yes, and he expressed to me he used to be one of my foster parents. It was an interesting moment when I was the very person who used to get abused, now investigating cases where children were getting abused. God has a way of turning the tables. That day was a defining moment. I was in that division for two years. Out of all the cases I worked, not one came across my desk that was worse than what I experienced, other than one child who died from his injuries.

One day, I had an epiphany. Someone helped me realize that I divorced a man I was with for eight years who treated me like a queen, yet I was with someone who treated me like crap for two years. I cut the cords quick and decided to stop listening to the lies. He was famous for giving what I called, "Martin Luther King speeches," but putting no action behind it. His time was up.

I wasn't good in the relationship arena. I made bad choices and rushed into commitment. I wanted to do the right thing, but would go about things the wrong way. I was finally figuring out that maybe the way Dad treated me did affect me. That was a reality I never wanted to face. I relied on my own strength and resilience to keep me. I knew I was strong and could make it through practically anything. It took a while before I connected the dots and realized I had poor judgment in men. Maybe there was a connection there, and all I had was me and God to get through it.

I got involved in another relationship. Although my mother forewarned me, I didn't listen. I wasn't used to listening to her for important things. I was just used to being on my own and doing things the way I felt they should have been done. The next few years taught me hard life's lessons. I never took the time to see how the relationship between me and my father not only affected my choice in men and my decisions, but it impacted me severely. What's worse than having a problem and not seeking any help? Not knowing you have a problem to begin with. It's also very dangerous to be in committed relationships with the wrong people who don't care for you as an individual. When you were your own worst enemy, you attract your enemy. Going through things that bring you pain can have you making wrong decisions if you aren't careful and clear. Everyone will make mistakes. One of the worst things to do is make important decisions that will affect the rest of your life, only to regret those decisions later.

After a few failed relationships, I realized I had been in a relationship or had a boyfriend ever since high school. I never took the time to heal, and I never took the time to get to know myself. I told myself I would be single for five years before I attempted getting into a relationship again.

Years passed where I felt hopeless. Family didn't feel like family, but God was working it all out. I went on to complete my bachelor's and master's degrees. I went from being a child protection detective to a robbery/homicide detective, with about seven years' experience as a detective in my 15 years of law enforcement. After over ten years with JPD, I pursued being a federal police officer and held that position for a few more years, until I retired from law enforcement. I set out on a God-given mission and founded Somebody Step In, Inc., a nonprofit organization for foster children/teens and adults who have been through adverse situations.

I once searched for my true purpose in life, now I know it's to share my story—to motivate and encourage others to reach beyond the break. All the relationships in my life, primarily with my husband, Paul Wesley Franks Jr., have been mended and are growing more and more daily. For that, I am thankful.

The memories I shared in this book are pivotal points in my life that helped me become the person I am today. This book does not cover every incident, just the most catastrophic ones. I can't explain why I experienced what I did; all I know is that it happened. Many years ago, I was told what someone thinks of you is not your business. That concept alone was very powerful and assisted me with putting my thoughts in proper perspective. I had no control over how Dad treated me, or any control over how life was for him when he was a child. All I had control over is how I would live the rest of my life. Would it be in misery? Would I stay upset and forever mad, or would I dust myself off, and create the life I wanted to live?

The next few pages list five steps that have helped me overcome the negative effects associated with going through challenging, painful situations. Each step is equally important. I hope this book will help you believe and know, no matter what has happened to you, there is a purpose and plan for your life. Someone you don't know is watching and admiring you. Be the light you were created to be. No one can take that from you.

Broken & Bruised

Five Steps to Overcoming Affliction

Step One: Get it Out

Cast thy burden upon the LORD, and he shall sustain thee: he shall never suffer the righteous to be moved.
(Psalm 55:22)

The very first time I shared my story, I told my high school best friends in twelfth grade. They both told me they never would have known. That was just the beginning, but it felt good to relieve the pressure built up over all those years. One day, I was driving down the street. I looked to my right at a basketball court where a man was playing with a little girl who I assumed was his daughter. As I glanced at them, I felt no emotion; everything was fine. He picked the little girl up as she held the basketball in her hands. He raised her to the hoop, and she dunked the ball in the hoop. Immediately, I broke down crying, wiping my face as I remembered I needed to see the road as I drove.

I talked about my story until I could finally talk about it without crying every single time. I shared my story for a purpose, whenever the opportunity presented itself. I don't recommend sharing your story with everyone. But share with someone who loves and cares about you. If you're in a place where you're not surrounded with family or loved ones, then try counselors, pastors or life coaches.

It's important to relieve the stress by talking about it and not keeping things bottled in. Whatever it takes for you to get closure with what happened and position yourself to get past it is what you need to do. Everyone is different; try different things until you get the results you need.

Step Two: Create New Habits of Thinking

But Jesus beheld them, and said unto them, with men this is impossible; but with God all things are possible. (Matthew 19:26)

Most of my life, I thought nothing would go right for me. My biggest hurdles were school, my career and my purpose. The way I viewed life was based off what I went through. Being talked down to and treated poorly, adversely affected by what I thought of myself. I grew up thinking this way for several years. I had to intentionally critique every thought I had until it was no longer instinctive for me to not believe in myself.

I didn't value myself or felt I was worthy of success. I learned the importance of both by educating myself and becoming affiliated with what I wanted to become.

My grandfather's last words gave me the motivation I needed. Because I valued my grandfather, therefore, I valued his words. There was a time when I was confused. I didn't know how to figure things out or how to be successful. When it came to a college degree, I would start well, but couldn't see how I would finish. I feel it was in part to being impatient, not thinking I had what it took to be consistent enough for four years or more. I decided to figure out how to make it happen.

I had to create new habits. One of those new habits was to make things simple. I started doing something to contribute to my goals every single day and stopped getting overwhelmed with the process by looking years down the road. Simply focusing on the current day made a world of difference. I was able to complete my associate's, bachelor's and my master's degrees.

When I would say, "I can't," I was speaking those words over my life. Now, there is no way I can if I just told myself I can't. There are some things you shouldn't allow yourself to say. There is power in the words we speak. Speak life, not only into others but to yourself. It can happen for you. It is possible.

Step Three: Be Intentionally Optimistic

Death and life are in the power the tongue: and they that love it shall eat the fruit thereof.
(Proverbs 18:21)

I found that writing and saying positive affirmations daily works wonders. It truly assists with reprogramming your way of thinking. When you take the garbage out of your brain, you must replace it with good things. You may never be able to change what happened, but you can change how you live your life moving forward.

I have seen, heard and read how people who were a victim of child abuse grew up to have kids, and they would abuse their children because that's what was done to them. I'm thankful I intentionally ensured this wouldn't get passed down to my children.

Oprah Winfrey, Lisa Nichols and Terri Savelle Foy are some of my greatest inspirations. Their stories of how they overcame obstacles and went on to live a better life inspire me daily. Stories are powerful.

Everything you want in life, speak it into existence. I am a huge fan of vision boards and although last year, I couldn't check everything off the list, I did check off some things. Speak positive words over your life and over your situation. You may have your ups and downs, but eventually you will get there.

Step Four: Forgive

For if ye forgive men their trespasses, your heavenly Father will also forgive you.
(Matthew 6:14)

I used to hate my parents. I thought I had forgiven them both, then I learned it wasn't true forgiveness. I didn't see them in their best light. It wasn't until I put myself in their shoes and even attempted to see things from their perspective was I ever truly able to forgive.

I looked at their lives and what it was like for them growing up in their era. Of course, as I got older and experienced life, I understood it wasn't so easy. No one is perfect. My mother is very delicate and stronger than ever; she did the best she could do with what she had at the time. While I don't condone my father's behavior, he had a story of his own. I learned my father was adopted. At age two, his mother put him in scalding hot water and gave him second and third-degree burns, which oftentimes causes psychological trauma. Knowing this assisted me in the area of compassion.

To this day, I don't understand why Dad treated me the way he did, but I love and care about my father. He's Dad. Every conversation we have, he always tells me his prayer is that we forgive him. Sometimes, my heart hurts for him. I know he didn't want things to turn out the way they did.

Recently, my mother told me she never intended for us (her

children) to go through the things we did. It did my heart good just hearing her say that. I know there were things I did in life. Looking back, on the front end I thought things would be perfect. Yet, I made mistakes of my own and learned how life works.

I talk to Dad, and he visits when he's in town. He calls me his number one. I know he regrets his past mistakes, and I pray he heals from them as well. The forgiveness process was a long, hard one for me. It didn't happen overnight. I just had to keep working on it until I got it right. I continuously search myself, my heart and mind to make sure there's no stone left unturned. By being unforgiving, it's hard to move on. You can't soar high with extra weight and baggage. Practicing forgiveness helps lighten your load. God can lift you higher and higher.

Step Five: Prayer/Meditation

The Lord is my shepherd; I shall not want. He maketh me to lie down in green pastures: he leadeth me beside the still waters. He restoreth my soul: he leadeth me in the paths of righteousness for his name's sake. Yea, though I walk through the valley of the shadow of death, I will fear no evil: for thou art with me; thy rod and thy staff they comfort me. Thou preparest a table before me in the presence of mine enemies: thou anointest my head with oil; my cup runneth over. Surely goodness and mercy shall follow me all the days of my life: and I will dwell in the house of the Lord forever.

(Psalm 23)

A short while ago, I went to a holistic doctor by the name of Kelly Englemann who owns the Wellness Center. This was a different approach, but I knew there were things going on with my body which needed a deeper look. I learned I was over-stressed, and had been living this way for years ever since childhood. I was educated on the importance of working out the right way for my body. Getting back to things such as yoga was a necessity. I worked extremely hard and thought I was doing all the right things. I was partaking in rigorous workout plans thinking it was the best thing to do; however, I was putting my body through more stress.

I've recently sought out a more efficient workout plan that's a good fit for my body, as well as incorporating yoga back into my life. I got so busy with work I had stopped making time for the important

74

things. I suggest you find out what it is your body needs, and develop a plan/system and work it.

I know prayer works. God has restored and is continuing to restore meaningful relationships in my life. God can fix it.

These steps don't have to be followed in the listed order. Whichever step you naturally gravitate towards should be where you start. There's no need to make the process any more difficult; however, the goal is that you come out a champion on the other side.

Share your story; you just may inspire someone not to give up who was thinking about throwing in the towel.

No More Flinching

The Merriam-Webster's definition of *flinching* is to draw back in fear, pain or disgust. I used to flinch uncontrollably. I would ball up my body, bracing myself for the impact. I expected it, and I knew it would hurt. It wasn't only a reaction I had with Dad, or people around me; it was my first reaction in life. I expected the pain to come. I flinched at the thought of having a bright future. I flinched at the thought of being able to complete my college degrees or being able to buy a house. Flinching was a way of life. I went through life, flinching mentally and physically, because I was so used to the pain.

God was with me through it all. It became clear to me as I sat in the back when I attended a random church. The pastor preached a message, and I felt like he was talking directly to me. He said, "The devil has been doing everything he can to kill you and destroy you. He's sent his best after you. Everything you set out to do, it seems like something always happens and nothing ever turns out right. The devil has been doing his best and you're still here!" The pastor explained that, in order for the devil to come after you with his absolute best, you must be stronger than you think. Obviously, God has a plan for your life. I hold onto those words as tightly as I hold on to my grandfather's words. It makes sense to me that maybe I just need to change the way I think.

I don't recall where I was, I just recall the feeling. Over a decade ago, someone reached into my personal space and their hand passed my face in my peripheral vision. My body triggered no unconscious reaction.

I shouted with joy, "I'm not flinching anymore!" I haven't flinched since.

Carlotta Taylor

About the Author

From foster care to living in too many shelters to count, depression and suicidal attempts, Carlotta Taylor, author and speaker, knows that it was nothing but the grace of God that kept her from jail, the streets or worse. Transferred from 26 various foster care homes because of abuse and neglect, she learned early on that if she didn't transform her mind, she would be consumed by the chaotic world around her. Realizing that nothing just happens—and that God uses even our suffering to be a blessing—Carlotta seeks to inspire others to press beyond their breaking point, even if she only touches one person.

Severely beaten by her father, and suffering mental, spiritual and physical abuse in the many foster homes she once resided in, Carlotta encourages people worldwide to know that their difficulties in life do not have to define their future. As a former homicide detective, child protection detective, and former federal officer, with over 15 years law enforcement experience, she knew she had to use her knowledge and wisdom to effect greater change in and around the community. As the founder of Somebody Step In, Inc., a non-profit for foster children, teens and young adults, she offers coaching and mentorship in education, life skills and more. Her extensive professional and personal background has opened doors for her to serve as a motivational speaker at schools, catholic charities and shelters. After having received three accommodation awards in law enforcement, even in her retirement, it is crystal clear that this is not just a career for her.

It's ministry.

After searching for her purpose for years, she soon learned that her purpose was to share her story and inspire others who may be going through what she endured and overcame triumphantly. And even though she's great at everything from makeup, hair and art— and even truck driving—she gets no greater fulfillment than that of walking someone through their healing process. Suddenly, life as she knew it all made sense. In her debut book, *No More Flinching*, Carlotta outlines five key steps to overcoming adversity. Flinching was the reaction she had right before her father oftentimes punched her in the face. But even after he and her mother divorced, the damage already done, she still flinched if someone reached for something near her. Until one day, it all stopped. *She didn't flinch anymore.* More importantly, she learned how to truly forgive her father.

Holding both a Bachelor of Arts in Social Services and a Master's in Science and Leadership from Belhaven University, Carlotta is using her educational, spiritual and emotional skill sets to host workshops under Somebody Step In, Inc., which will include goal setting, journaling, gear and gift cards to attendees. With her strong spirit of discernment, clear vision about the future, wit and love for others, she's committed to kicking procrastination to the curb and shining her light brightly for all to see. And she encourages others to do the same.

For more information, booking, or speaking engagements email

cdtgroupllc@gmail.com

or

www.nomoreflinching.com

Made in the USA
Lexington, KY
22 September 2019